LIFE ON AN APPLE ORCHARD

LIFE ON AN APPLE ORCHARD

by Judy Wolfman
photographs by David Lorenz Winston

LIFE ON A
FARM

Carolrhoda Books, Inc. / Minneapolis

Our thanks and appreciation to David, Sharon, Julie, Keith, and Emily Hodge, for sharing their time and their knowledge about apples with us.   —J.W. and D.L.W.

Text copyright © 2004 by Judy Wolfman
Photographs copyright © 2004 by David Lorenz Winston

Carolrhoda Books, Inc.
A division of Lerner Publishing Group
241 First Avenue North
Minneapolis, MN 55401 U.S.A.

Website address: www.lernerbooks.com

Library of Congress Cataloging-in-Publication Data

Wolfman, Judy.
    Life on an apple orchard / by Judy Wolfman ; photographs by David Lorenz Winston.
        p.   cm. — (Life on a farm)
    Summary: A child explains the activities that take place at home on a working apple orchard.
    ISBN: 1–57505–193–1 (lib. bdg. : alk. paper)
    1. Apples—Juvenile literature. 2. Orchards—Juvenile literature. 3. Farm life—Juvenile literature. [1. Apples. 2. Orchards. 3. Farm life.]
    I. Title: Apple orchard. II. Winston, David Lorenz, ill. III. Title.
    SB363.W76 2004
    634'.11—dc21   2002152920

Manufactured in the United States of America
1 2 3 4 5 6 – DP – 09 08 07 06 05 04

CONTENTS

WELCOME
to Highland
✿ Orchards

I like living and working on an apple orchard with my family.

When most people want an apple, they go to their refrigerators or to the store. But when my family wants apples, we go to our orchard and pick them! To me, nothing tastes better than a fresh, crisp, juicy apple.

I'm Emily Hodge, and I live on a fruit farm with my parents, my older brother, Keith, and my younger sister, Julie. Our farm is called Highland Orchards. We think it's a fun and beautiful place to live. On our farm, we grow a variety of vegetables and fruit, but we mostly grow apples. We grow twenty-seven different kinds!

6

I love to help out in the bakery. Can you guess why?

At our market, people can buy our crispy apples whenever they like.

On our farm, we have a market, or store. This is where people can buy our apples and delicious apple foods all year round. At the bakery there, we use our fruit to make pies, too. They taste as good as they smell!

My dad's grandparents started the farm a long time ago. Then his parents took it over. Now Dad and two of his brothers run it, with the help of some workers during harvesttime. And when we kids aren't in school, we do as much as we can.

Growing apples is a lot of work. We have jobs to do during every season. But the work we do during the winter is really important. It helps the rest of the year go smoothly.

In the winter, apple trees are bare. They have no leaves, no flowers, and no apples. The trees are sleeping, so they can grow luscious apples later.

One acre is about the size of a football field. We farm 350 acres!

These trees will have lots of work to do when the weather warms up.

Dad prunes to help get the trees ready for growing apples.

Dad works around the orchard during this time. He **prunes**, or trims, the trees by sawing off branches and limbs. This makes the trees the right shape and height. That way, when the leaves start to grow in the spring, they will get lots of sunlight. Sunlight helps apples grow big and healthy.

Dad also looks for older trees that need to be cut down. When a tree gets to be twenty to twenty-five years old, its fruit is not as colorful or as big as it used to be. Bigger apples sell better than smaller ones do, so it's best to take out these older trees. We cut down the trees and remove the stumps and roots. Then we cut the trees into logs and sell them for firewood.

Soon the sun shines brighter, the weather gets warmer, and we get busier.

Sunshine helps apple trees to start blooming.

APPLE
Growing Begins

When spring comes, growing season starts. First Dad checks the trees again and prunes the ones that still need it. Then he cleans up the limbs and brush that lie on the ground. He also spreads **fertilizer** under the trees. Fertilizer helps plants grow.

Spring is also a time to plant. In some of the places where we took out old trees, we plant **seedlings**, or young trees. We buy seedlings at a nursery, a place where plants are grown and sold. To make a seedling, a nursery worker takes a small branch from a healthy apple tree. Then the worker joins it together with a strong root of another apple tree. This seedling grows for about two years. Then it is finally big enough to plant. After it's planted, we have to wait about three *more* years before the tree grows apples.

When my great-grandfather started the orchard, he planted trees 40 feet apart.
We plant them closer, so we have more trees per acre.

During these warm months, Dad mows the tall grass. Keeping the grass cut makes it easier for us to harvest our apples in the fall. Mowing also helps keep pests away from our trees, so they can't hurt them.

At this time, bugs seem to burst out of hibernation. In our apple orchard, we have helpful bugs and not-so-helpful bugs. The "bad" bugs, such as mites and worms, can hurt our fruit and our trees. The "good" bugs, like black ladybugs, eat the bad bugs. We like to keep these good bugs around!

14

It's fun to see the trees get greener and fuller with leaves. Bugs like this time of year, too.

I like to help Dad look for the bad bugs. If they have done damage to a tree, we want to find out!

To help our apple trees stay healthy, Dad works to get rid of the bad bugs. I help Dad by going with him to look for bugs or diseases they've caused. We look like detectives as we check out leaves with our magnifying glasses. If we see orange-and-black spots underneath a leaf or find a leaf that's curled up, we know that bad bugs are to blame.

16

First Dad tries to get rid of the bugs with glue traps. Most of the time the traps work just fine, but sometimes they don't. When this happens, Dad uses a spray that usually helps take care of the bugs once and for all. Dad doesn't like to use chemicals unless he has to.

Our sticky glue traps catch a lot of bugs each spring.

The weather gets warmer in April. The **buds** on the trees begin to grow. (A bud is a small swelling on a plant that develops into a flower.) This is the time when Dad and a beekeeper bring about fifty beehives into the orchard. The beehives are filled with lots of honeybees! The bees buzz around and wait for the buds to open up into flowers.

When Dad opens the beehive, he has to be careful. Bees can sting!

These bees can't wait to start buzzing around the flowers. It won't be long now.

Once the trees start to bloom, our orchard looks like a giant flower garden.

I think these tiny flowers are beautiful.

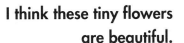

Toward the end of April, the buds become full-grown, and the blossoms finally begin to open. Before long, the orchard is full of groups, or clusters, of beautiful white flowers. Each cluster has five blossoms. (Each blossom can grow an apple.) Four small ones grow around a large one, called the **king blossom**. The king blossom will grow a bigger apple than the others.

19

Bees work hard at pollination! Soon this bloom will form into a small apple.

Once the flowers are all open, they need help from the honeybees. These bees help the blossoms grow into apples. This is how it works: Each bee looks for **nectar** to drink. Nectar is a sweet liquid in a flower. As a bee looks, it rubs against **pollen.**

Pollen is a yellowish powder inside a flower. When the bee travels, it carries the pollen from one flower to another. This process, called **pollination**, begins an apple's life. It's exciting to watch bees buzz around our orchard!

Honeybees work best in warm, sunny weather. But if the weather is below 60 degrees, or windy or rainy, the bees won't pollinate. Bees don't fly well with raincoats and goggles! If the bees don't pollinate, we won't get a good **crop** (or harvest) of apples.

If it weren't for bees and pollination, we wouldn't have any apples.

I do what I can to help Dad. This tree
needs trimming.

After the bees pollinate the flowers,
Dad thins out the blossoms. To do this,
he snips off the four little ones with scis-
sors. That way, the king blossom can
grow better. This job is important,
because it helps the king blossom to
grow into a big, juicy apple!

22

Soon our apples start to grow. All young apples are small and green at first. To stay healthy and grow well, apples need plenty of sun. If it rains a lot, the apple trees may drink too much water. If this happens, the apples may not look as pretty as usual. But if we don't get enough rain, apples may be smaller, and the trees could be damaged. This means that a good crop may not grow the next year. We always hope for just the right amount of rain.

These apples are not quite ready to pick.

In late June, the apple blossoms that were not pollinated drop off the tree on their own. We call this the **June drop**. June is also the month our school year ends. Our busy part of the season doesn't start for a while, so we usually take a family vacation during this time.

As our apples grow and grow, we get ready for the apple-picking season. We'll have lots of work soon. That's why Dad makes sure his workers are ready to go. Some of the workers Dad hires live nearby, but many come from Mexico. These workers live in homes that are near the orchard.

These apples are waiting to be picked.

When people think of apples, they usually think of red ones. But apples can be green, yellow, and pink, too.

By late summer, most of our apples are finally full-grown and are ready to be picked. Then we all have lots of fun picking, sorting, selling, and tasting our apples!

This apple looks perfect for picking!

Time for HARVEST

By **mid-September and early October, our orchard is full of big, beautiful apples.** This is called harvesttime. During these months, we kids help the workers do lots of jobs. One of our most important jobs is to pick apples.

I start by picking the apples I can reach. This is pretty easy, since all of our trees are **dwarfed**, or made small (they're only about 10 feet tall).

With a little stretching, I can fill my basket in no time at all!

When I'm ready to pick the apples that grow higher than I can reach, I use a short ladder. I lean the ladder against the tree, carefully climb up, and reach for the apple.

Before I pull an apple from the tree, I make sure it's **ripe.** A ripe apple is one that's ready for picking. I have lots of different ways to tell when an apple is ripe.

One test is to look at the color near the base of the stem. When I see yellow around the stem, I know the apple is probably ready to pick. (On a yellow apple, you can see a lighter yellow color around the base.)

Apples are a healthy fruit to eat.
Some people call them "glow fruits,"
because they're good for your skin.

Our customers love to buy our big, juicy apples—they're everyone's favorite.

I can tell this apple is ripe, because it tastes so good!

Another good test is to see how easy it is to take the apple off the branch. A ripe apple pulls off easily. The test I like best is the taste test—yummy! But the one I count on is Dad's word. He tells me which ones are ready, and he's usually right!

I can adjust the basket's strap so the basket is off to one side or in front of me.

When I think an apple is ready, I hold it gently and twist it. Then I pull it toward me until it breaks away from the branch. I put it into a basket that I strap onto my shoulder. When the basket is filled, it's heavy (over 20 pounds) and hard to carry. Finally, I put the basket onto a truck.

Sometimes my back gets sore after we load all the baskets onto the truck. They're heavy!

After these apples finish their ride on the conveyor belt, they will go to our market.

When the truck is loaded, we take the apples to our packinghouse. There the apples are prepared for selling. First we wash all the apples. Then we pick out the ones that are damaged. (Some may have cuts or bruises on them.)

We put the damaged ones in a special bin—they will be used to make apple cider. The good apples go on a **conveyor belt**, so we can sort and box them by size as the belt carries them past us.

Next we **grade** those apples. We put the highest-quality apples into boxes. We sell these to our customers right away or put them into **cold storage**. Cold storage is a room with a temperature between 29 to 32 degrees. It makes me shiver when I go in there, but it smells yummy—like fresh apples. In cold storage, the apples stay crisp and juicy. We can sell them all year round.

Inside the packinghouse, we sort and box our apples.

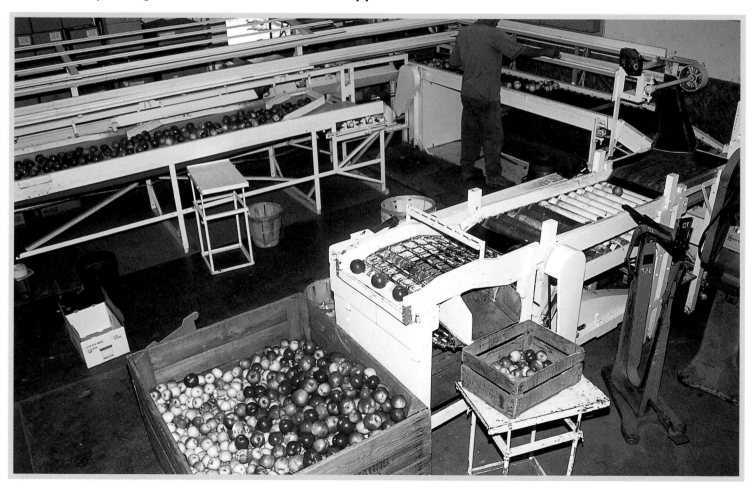

Our apples stay fresh in cold storage all through the winter. If I'm looking for a snack, sometimes I go into the cold-storage room and nibble on an apple.

During harvesttime, we like to decorate the outside of our market.

Some of our apples are shipped to canneries where applesauce is made. Others are sent to companies that make apple pies. We also sell our apples to local grocery stores and to schools.

During harvesttime, our orchard is buzzing with activities. We open our orchard to kids and adults. They can pick apples, visit our market, and take tours. It makes us feel good when we share our orchard with other people in the community.

Our sign tells people when they can pick their own apples at our orchard.

We welcome customers who want to pick apples from our trees. Before they start, I show them which trees they can pick from. I also put up signs that say "Do Not Pick These" in some areas.

If people don't see the signs and pick from any tree they like, I show them to the right ones. When customers finish picking the apples, they go to our market and pay for them.

Children have fun picking their own
pumpkins and taking apples home.

Some people pick lots and
lots of apples from our trees!

Busloads of school kids visit us, too. This is Mom's busy time, because she's in charge of the tours. The students ride a tractor-pulled hay wagon into the orchard. They get to see the varieties of apples, learn how to pick them, and take three apples home with them. Every child can also pick a gourd or mini pumpkin, and every classroom gets a big pumpkin.

We use this bus to drive lots of kids through our orchard.

During harvesttime, kids also have fun making stuffed scarecrows. And they like our maze of hay bales and crates that my brother, Keith, designs. Most kids really enjoy our animal section, too. They meet Jake the llama, Dandy the donkey, and other unusual animals.

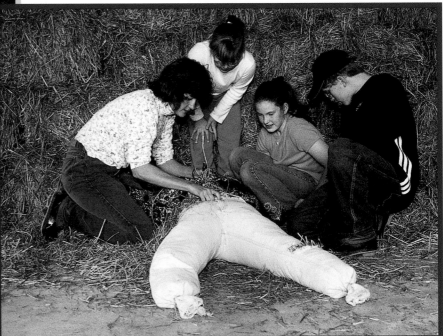

We make our own scarecrows and help other kids make theirs, too.

We have a great variety of apples. It doesn't take long before these baskets are empty. Then we have to fill them up again.

After Halloween, things slow down for us, and fewer people visit our orchard. This is the time when the weather gets colder and we pick our last varieties of apples for the year. Like other good apples we picked during the season, we put these apples in cold storage. Then we can sell them during the winter.

In November, Dad brings in the equipment from the orchard. He makes sure everything works properly for next spring. He mows the lawn one last time, too. Before we know it, winter comes and it's time to start all over again.

The year is almost over. The weather gets colder, and winter gets closer.

Keith, Julie, and I enjoy our lives on an apple orchard. We think it's interesting and fun—and always busy! We love to stand in the middle of the orchard and look down the long rows of trees. It's beautiful and quiet. We usually hear bees buzzing and birds chirping. And if we want a snack, we just reach up and pick the apple we want. Julie likes the slightly tart Jonagold best. Mom and Dad prefer the hard, rich Mutsu, but Keith and I like the sweet Gala. Our customers seem to like Red Delicious best.

We label our apples, so our customers know which kinds they're buying.

I'm proud to live and work in an apple orchard. We grow and sell fruit that almost everybody loves. I hope to always work in the orchard, but I don't ever want to run it. That's too much work! Keith thinks he might take over someday, and if he does, I'd like to work with him. In the meantime, I'll just enjoy living here and eating all the apples I want!

We love living on our apple orchard!

Fun Facts about APPLES

Presidents *George Washington* and *Thomas Jefferson* owned apple orchards.

THE AVERAGE AMERICAN EATS ABOUT **65 FRESH APPLES** EVERY YEAR.
THAT'S ALMOST 20 POUNDS OF APPLES!

There are 7,500 kinds of apples grown throughout the world.

SOME APPLE TREES LIVE
FOR MORE THAN ONE
HUNDRED YEARS!

The "Big Apple" is a nickname for New York City.

The largest apple ever picked weighed **3 pounds.** That's as heavy as a basketball!

APPLES are members of the **ROSE FAMILY** of plants, along with pears, peaches, and plums.

THE SCIENCE OF APPLE GROWING IS CALLED POMOLOGY.

Learn
More
about
APPLES

Books

Micucci, Charles. *The Life and Times of the Apple.* New York: Orchard Books, 1992. This book is packed with information about apples. You'll learn about the life of an apple and the history of this delicious fruit.

Patent, Dorothy Hinshaw. *Apple Trees.* Minneapolis, MN: Lerner Publications Company, 1997. Full-color photographs and lots of great information about apple trees fill this book. Read how the trees grow apples, and how apples get from a tree branch to your local supermarket!

Wallace, Nancy Elizabeth. *Apples, Apples, Apples.* New York: Winslow Press, 2000. This picture book takes you through a rabbit family's apple-picking adventure. You'll also find a recipe for applesauce, an apple craft, and a silly apple song.

Websites

Apples & More
<www.urbanext.uiuc.edu/apples>
Read about apple facts, apple varieties, how to preserve apples, and how to make apple cider. Follow links to other apple sites and learn about the life cycle of an apple tree, apple history and legends, and apple growing.

Apple Promotion Board of Maryland
<www.marylandapples.org>
Visit the Kid's Corner, and you'll find the story of Johnny Appleseed, yummy apple recipes, and a coloring book of apple characters. This site also has links to other great sites that include fun games, apple crafts, and steps to build your own corn maze.

Pennsylvania Apples
<www.paapples.org/consumer.htm>
Learn all about apples grown in Pennsylvania, their health benefits, and how to create delicious desserts with this sweet, juicy fruit.

Washington Apples
<www.bestapples.com/kids>
Created by the Washington State Apple Commission, this colorful site is loaded with goodness! You'll find information about the history of Washington apples, apple nutrition and recipes, and stories from kids who live on apple orchards.

GLOSSARY

buds: small swellings on a plant that develop into flowers

cold storage: a sealed room that has a temperature of 29 to 32 degrees. This room helps apples stay fresh.

conveyor belt: a mechanical device that moves things from one place to another

crop: a group of plants grown for food

dwarfed: kept from growing big or tall

fertilizer: a chemical mix, or animal waste, put on soil to help plants grow

grade: to group apples of the same quality

June drop: when unpollinated blossoms drop off a tree

king blossom: a large apple blossom that opens first in the center of a cluster of blossoms

nectar: a sweet liquid that flowers produce

orchard: a piece of land where fruit is grown

pollen: a fine, yellowish powder formed in flowers

pollination: moving pollen from one flower to another, causing seeds and fruits to grow. Pollen is moved by birds or insects such as honeybees.

prunes: trims branches off a tree

ripe: ready to be picked

seedlings: young trees

INDEX

About the AUTHOR

Judy Wolfman is a writer and professional story-teller who teaches workshops on storytelling, creativity, and writing. She also enjoys writing and acting for the theater. She has published three children's plays, numerous magazine articles, short stories, poems, finger plays, and Carolrhoda's *Life on a Farm* series. A retired schoolteacher, Ms. Wolfman has two sons, a daughter, and four granddaughters. She lives in York, Pennsylvania.

About the PHOTOGRAPHER

David Lorenz Winston is an award-winning photographer whose work has been published by *National Geographic World,* UNICEF, and the National Wildlife Federation. In addition to his work on the *Life on a Farm* series, Mr. Winston has been photographing pigs, cows, and other animals for many years. He lives in southeastern Pennsylvania. To learn more about Mr. Winston's work, visit his website at <http://www.davidlorenzwinston.com>.